# The Coming Judgment

## Based on Your Deeds

Harold R. Eberle

**Worldcast Publishing**
**Yakima, Washington, USA**

**The Coming Judgment Based on Your Deeds**

© 2011 by Harold R. Eberle
First printing, May 2011

Worldcast Publishing
P.O. Box 10653
Yakima, WA 98909-1653
(509) 248-5837
www.worldcastpublishing.com
office@worldcastpublishing.com

ISBN 978-1-882523-39-9
Cover by Lynette Brannan

Unless otherwise stated, all biblical quotations taken from the NEW AMERICAN STANDARD BIBLE®, Copyright © 1960, 1962, 1963, 1968, 1971, 1972, 1973, 1975, 1977, 1995 by The Lockman Foundation. Used by permission.

No part of this publication may be reproduced, stored in a retrieval system, or transmitted in any form or by any means—electronic, mechanical, photocopy, recording, or otherwise—without the express prior permission of Worldcast Publishing Company, with the exception of brief excerpts in magazine articles and/or reviews.

Requests for translating into other languages should be addressed to Worldcast Publishing.

Printed in the United States of America

# Table of Contents

Introduction ........................................................................... 1

  1. All-or-Nothing Salvation? ............................................ 3
  2. Defining Grace ............................................................ 7
  3. Defining Faith ........................................................... 13
  4. Defining Salvation .................................................... 19
  5. Good Deeds Are Good ............................................... 23
  6. Jesus' Righteousness Credited to Us ...................... 27
  7. The Individual Christian's Righteousness ............. 31
  8. Relational, Not Legal, Understanding ..................... 37
  9. Not All Sins Are Equal .............................................. 41
  10. A Works-Oriented Life ............................................ 45

Conclusion ............................................................................ 49
Other Books by Harold R. Eberle .......................................... 55

# Introduction

Christian thought has developed over the course of 2,000 years. As great thinkers faced the challenges of their times, they studied the Bible, debated the issues and added their insights. Leaders such as Augustine, Aquinas, Luther and Calvin profoundly impacted the thought patterns which we Christians share.

Of course all Christians bring their own unique perspectives. They read their Bible, reason about the issues and piece together a picture of how the world around them operates. In particular, they arrive at conclusions about God and His involvement in this world. The resulting thought patterns are one's theology.

Right or wrong, each person has a theology.

Christians like to think that their theology has been developed from the Bible. However, many Christians have had the experience of reading through the Bible and finding specific passages which do not seem to fit into their theological understanding. At that moment they must ignore the contradictory passages or question their own theology.

This dilemma confronts many Christians when they read Bible passages which talk about a future judgment based on deeds. The reason those Bible passages are troublesome is because their theological understanding leads them to believe that they are saved by grace, and they define grace as God's unmerited favor. If, indeed, God's favor is totally unmerited, then there are no deeds which will earn God's rewards. Some

# The Coming Judgment Based on Your Deeds

Christians have a difficult time accepting a future judgment based on deeds because their theology tells them that future judgment is *only* based on their acceptance or rejection of Jesus Christ.

Some Christians have reconciled the significance of deeds and the truth that we are saved by grace, but most simply think about the varying ideas at different times. One day they will read the Scriptures about judgments and rewards, but on another day they will think about Jesus being their righteousness and, therefore, the only basis on which they will be judged. They can hold opposing views because they don't think about them at the same time.

I can't do that. If my theology does not allow me to understand certain Bible passages, then I need to re-evaluate my theology. More importantly, if my deeds are going to be taken into account on judgment day, then I want to know—now. Just like a student in school wants to know what is going to be on a test before he or she takes it, I want to know what is going to be on the test on judgment day.

This book offers those answers.

I will start each chapter with a passage from the New Testament which talks about a future judgment based on deeds. Then I will address some aspect of our theology which must be adjusted to reconcile the future judgment based on deeds with the truth that we are saved by grace through faith. In the process we will discover what is going to be on our final exam.

## Chapter 1

# All-or-Nothing Salvation?

**Jesus' Teaching about the Judgment Based on Deeds:**

Jesus described judgment day as a day when the sheep will be separated from the goats (Matt. 25:31-33). Then He explained the basis for that separation:

> *"Then the King will say to those on His right, 'Come, you who are blessed of My Father, inherit the kingdom prepared for you from the foundation of the world. For I was hungry, and you gave Me something to eat; I was thirsty, and you gave Me something to drink; I was a stranger, and you invited Me in; naked, and you clothed Me; I was sick, and you visited me; I was in prison, and you came to Me.'"*
>
> (Matt. 25:34-36)

When asked for further explanation, Jesus said,

> *"Truly I say to you, to the extent that you did it to one of these brothers of Mine, even the least of them, you did it to Me."*
>
> (Matt. 25:40)

# The Coming Judgment Based on Your Deeds

According to Jesus' explanation, judgment will be based on our actions—in particular, our actions toward our oppressed and disadvantaged brothers and sisters.

## Adjusting Our Theology:

Many Christians cannot accept these words of Jesus about a future judgment based on deeds. The primary reason is because they have an *all-or-nothing understanding of salvation*. Their theology tells them that God placed all judgment upon Jesus and, therefore, there will be no future judgment based on our deeds. They reason that the righteousness of Jesus belongs to every Christian and, therefore, we will each be rewarded according to all that belongs to Jesus. They think of every human being as:

- Saved or not saved;
- Reconciled to God or separated from God;
- Righteous or unrighteous;
- Going to heaven or going to hell;
- Receiving all of God's rewards or none of God's rewards.

This all-or-nothing understanding of salvation leaves no room for a future judgment based on deeds.

This understanding was seated into Protestant Christianity during the Protestant Reformation. Protestant leaders saw the Roman Catholic Church as a works-oriented religion, wrongly teaching people that they would have to work to earn God's rewards. Rejecting the related teachings, Protestants took great efforts to distinguish their beliefs from those of Catholicism.

I am not a Roman Catholic. But there is something wrong with the theology of us Protestants. We have so emphasized the truth of salvation by grace through faith that we cannot

## All-or-Nothing Salvation?

fit into our theology the Bible passages which talk about the role of deeds in a future judgment. Perhaps our Protestant forefathers were so determined to distinguish their teachings from Roman Catholicism that the pendulum swung too far. We now have a theology that does not allow us to believe the words of Jesus that judgment will take into account how we cared for the hungry, thirsty, stranger, naked, sick and imprisoned (Matt. 25:34-40).

For us to seriously consider the role of deeds, we must re-evaluate our all-or-nothing understanding of salvation. This is no small task. To question the fundamental doctrine of salvation established during the Protestant Reformation is to step into the lion's den. Many Christians are so defensive of this one doctrine that they would never even consider questioning it. For many, this is the one doctrine that distinguishes true Christians from false believers. Those holding tightly to an all-or-nothing understanding of salvation will label any contrary teaching as "works-oriented religion." Some quickly associate works-oriented religion with Roman Catholics, Jehovah Witnesses, Mormons or some other sect which they have already judged negatively.

It is especially Christians who have been trained in Reformed theology (the teachings of John Calvin) who are defensive of the all-or-nothing understanding of salvation. Therefore, I will refer to the teachings of John Calvin in coming pages. Historians recognize Calvin as the father of Reformed theology, which only represents a portion of the theological thinking developed during the Protestant Reformation. However, Calvin's theology profoundly influenced all of Protestant Christianity.

There is no doubt: we have been saved by grace through faith. This is a simple, clear statement of the gospel. However, we need to look carefully at the meaning of this truth. Only by having an accurate understanding of salvation will

# The Coming Judgment Based on Your Deeds

we be able to see the proper place for deeds. So then, we will examine each word in this gospel statement: first we will look at "grace," then "faith" and then "saved."

## Chapter 2
# Defining Grace

### Paul Talking about the Judgment Seat of Christ:

The apostle Paul wrote:

> *For we must all appear before the judgment seat of Christ, so that each one may be recompensed for his deeds in the body, according to what he has done, whether good or bad.*
>
> (II Cor. 5:10)

In the context of this passage Paul is talking to Christians. Yes, we Christians will all stand before the judgment seat of Christ.

I have heard some Christian teachers try explain away the clear meaning of this passage. Wanting to hold to their all-or-nothing theology of salvation, they say that the judgment seat of Christ is a place where Christians will only receive awards. They say it will be like an awards banquet and there will be no negative judgments for Christians.

But that explanation does not work because Paul ended by saying each person will *"be recompensed for his deeds in the body, according to what he has done, whether good or bad."*

# The Coming Judgment Based on Your Deeds

## **Adjusting Our Theology:**

For you and I to accept these words about judgment, we are going to have to question the all-or-nothing understanding of salvation. As we re-evaluate, we will see how certain words and concepts were defined during the Protestant Reformation in ways that reinforce the all-or-nothing understanding of salvation.

For example, consider the word, "grace." Most Christians define grace as "unmerited favor." This is one traditionally accepted definition. In reality, this definition of grace as "unmerited favor" is weak and misleading. This is true for several reasons.

First, "favor" can mean something as simple as an act of kindness. Certainly, salvation is an act of kindness, but you and I were saved by *more* than a simple act of kindness. We were saved by God acting in history, sending His Son into the world, giving His life on the cross, resurrecting Him from the dead, ascending Him above all rule and authority, and then giving us access to His divine nature and pouring His Spirit into us. Once we note this, we can see why "favor" does not say enough.

The word "grace" in the New Testament is translated from the Greek word, *charis*. Strong's Bible Concordance (#5463) defines grace as "the divine influence upon the heart, and its reflection in the life." This definition is adequate in some contexts, but in the context of salvation it gives no recognition to all that God did through the death, resurrection and ascension of His Son. Grace is more than a divine influence. It is what God does in the heart of an individual, but it is also all that God does outside of the person to make salvation possible. For a more accurate definition we can say that grace is God's blessings, help, love, power, nature and Spirit freely given to us.

## Defining Grace

> Grace is God's blessings, help, love, power, nature and Spirit freely given to us.

Now think again of the traditional definition of grace as "unmerited favor." Another problem with this definition is that there is no justification for adding the word "unmerited" onto the definition of grace. I stated that grace refers to all that God has freely given to us, but freely given is not equivalent to "unmerited." When I say the first, "freely given," I am referring to something God does. When I say, "unmerited," I am referring to actions or behavior which the recipient of the grace does or does not do. In reality, what the recipient does or does not do is irrelevant to the definition of grace.

To see this more clearly, let's say I am going to give a present to someone. As I give the present I could say, "Here is the gift." Or I could say, "Here is the unmerited gift." Notice that adding the word, "unmerited" is unnecessary and adds information which is not essential to the definition of "gift."

So why do many Christians add the word, "unmerited" to their definition of grace? Because Christians who developed this definition could use it to reinforce their all-or-nothing theology of salvation. Using the word "unmerited" they implied that no one can do anything to merit salvation. However, notice that it is a circular argument to define grace as unmerited favor and then say that no one can merit it.

The more significant problem is that if we tack on the word unmerited, too many Christians take this to mean that people are completely and totally passive as God gives grace. Yet, many Bible passages talk about an active role humans can play with God's grace.

The writer of Hebrews tells us to approach the throne of grace in order that we may *"find grace to help in time of need"* (Heb. 4:16). Here we see grace as God's help freely given to us, but we can play a role in going to Him to receive His grace. Similarly we can read how God *"gives grace to the humble"* (James 4:6). The humble do not merit God's grace, but there is something people can do—humble themselves—which results in their being given grace. Furthermore, Paul encourages us to *"receive the abundance of grace"* (Rom. 5:17), meaning there is some part we play—receiving—in the grace which we experience.

Teachers of Reformed theology not only say God's grace is unmerited, but it is also irresistible. By this they mean that people have no choice nor ability to resist doing what God gave the grace to do. Yet, the Bible gives us several examples which contradict this understanding of grace. For example, Paul exhorts the Corinthian Christians *"not to receive the grace of God in vain"* (II Cor. 6:1), something which would be impossible if the Reformed understanding of grace was true. In another passage Paul and Barnabus urged their listeners to *"continue in the grace of God"* (Acts 13:43), which would be a foolish exhortation if grace was irresistible. The writer of Hebrews tells his readers not to fall short of the grace of God (Heb. 12:15) and Peter tells his listeners to be *"good stewards of the manifold grace of God"* (II Peter 4:10), both of which show people as active participants with the grace of God.

Passages like these reveal how certain Protestant reformers developed their definition of grace from their all-or-nothing theology, rather than start with the Bible and accept the definition of grace as used by the Bible writers.

Adjusting our definition of grace changes our understanding of deeds. If we understand grace to be *God's blessings, help, love, power, nature and Spirit freely given to us,* then we can understand how grace enables us to do good deeds. An excellent example is Paul who wrote how he labored according to the grace given to him (I Cor. 15:10). The grace was freely given to him, but Paul still labored to fulfill God's will for his life. Similarly, we are encouraged to work according to the grace given to us (Rom. 12:6).

## Chapter 3

# Defining Faith

### Paul Talking about the Judgment Seat of God:

I started the last chapter quoting Paul's words about how we will all stand before the judgment seat of Christ. Some teachers try to separate the judgment seat of Christ from the judgment seat of God, and then they say that Christians will stand before the judgment seat of Christ, while non-Christians will be judged at the judgment seat of God.

That distinction does not hold up under examination. In another passage Paul tells us that we Christians will all stand before the *judgment seat of God*:

> *But you, why do you judge your brother? Or you again, why do you regard your brother with contempt? For we will all stand before the judgment seat of God. For it is written,*
> *"As I live, says the Lord, every knee shall bow to Me,*
> *And every tongue shall give praise to God."*
> *So then each one of us will give an account of himself to God.*
> (Rom. 14:10-12)

Make no mistake that this passage is a warning to "brothers," that is, Christians. We will all stand before the judgment seat

# The Coming Judgment Based on Your Deeds

of God and give an account.

We cannot separate the judgment seat of God from the judgment seat of Christ. Jesus declared that God the Father gave all judgment over to the Son:

> *For not even the Father judges anyone, but He has given all judgment to the Son.*
> (John 5:22)

There may be different *times* when individuals are judged. Some Christian teachers understand Revelation 20 as indicating two different judgments. But whether or not there is one judgment or more, there is only one judgment throne and Jesus sits on that throne.

This book is not about the timing of the judgment(s). Instead, we are focusing on the truth pertaining to how all people—including Christians—will be judged. More importantly, we want to discover the basis on which Christians will be judged.

Paul wrote that at the judgment seat of God each Christian will:

> *give an account of himself to God.*
> (Rom. 14:12)

At the judgment seat of Christ each Christian will:

> *be recompensed for his deeds in the body, according to what he has done, whether good or bad.*
> (II Cor. 5:10)

We cannot escape this fact that Paul (and Jesus) describe a future judgment day when our deeds, good and bad, will be taken into account.

## Adjusting Our Theology:

If we are going to fit into our understanding the place of deeds in the future judgment, we are going to have to consider more carefully the gospel statement: "we are saved by grace through faith."

Each preposition in this gospel statement is important. Note that we are saved *by* grace. We are not saved by faith. In other words, faith does not save us. It is God's grace that saves us. However, that grace comes to us *through* faith.

Allow me to offer a helpful illustration showing the relationship between grace and faith. Compare the grace of God to the heat flowing from the sun toward the earth. If you and I stand out in the sunlight we will be warmed by the sunlight. We receive the warmth *through* our skin. This is comparable to how we receive grace *through* faith. Our skin does not warm us, but the sunlight does. Nor does our faith save us, but grace does. Faith is the avenue through which we receive God's grace.

But we Christians in Western society tend to have a distorted understanding of "faith." One reason is because we read the Bible through the Western worldview, which has its foundation in ancient Greek thought pattens. At the foundation of our thought patterns is a division which separates the spiritual realm from the natural realm. Even today, we read the Bible through this paradigm.[1]

One result of our Western worldview is that we tend to think of faith as belonging to the spiritual realm while deeds belong to the natural realm. As a consequence, we separate the spiritual exercise of faith from the natural exercise of works (or doing good deeds).

In reality, the Bible was written with a Hebrew worldview,

---

[1] For a more complete discussion of this Western tendency to separate the spiritual from the natural, see my book, entitled, *Christianity Unshackled*.

# The Coming Judgment Based on Your Deeds

which sees the spiritual and natural realms as totally integrated. A truly biblical understanding leads one to believe that what a person does in the spiritual realm is inseparable from what a person does in the natural realm. Simply stated, faith and deeds are inseparable.

With this understanding, James wrote, *"faith without works is dead"* (James 2:26). James gave us an example of how living faith produces good works:

> *If a brother or sister is without clothing and in need of daily food, and one of you says to them, "Go in peace, be warmed and be filled," and yet you do not give them what is necessary for their body, what use is that? Even so faith, if it has not works, is dead, being by itself.*
>
> (James 2:15-17)

This concept is easy to understand if we read the Bible through the Hebrew worldview in which it was written. True faith—that is, faith that is alive—produces good works.

It takes a conscious effort for Western-minded people to fully grasp this. They may try to link faith and works, but even then they tend to subconsciously keep them in two separate compartments.

This is especially difficult for Protestant Christians because of the heritage handed to us by our Protestant forefathers. Our forefathers had a Western worldview that separated the spiritual and natural realms. But they also were trying to distinguish their teaching from those of Roman Catholicism. In their attempt to make their point they forced a greater separation between faith and works.

In reality, they should have been content to separate grace from faith. If they had made it clear that we are saved by grace, rather than faith, then they could have left faith and

## Defining Faith

works associated, as they are meant to be.

Faith does not save us. Even faith with works does not save us. Only God's grace saves us. We receive that grace through faith. The faith that receives God's grace is the same faith that produces a lifestyle of good works.

## Chapter 4
# Defining Salvation

### Judgment According to Spoken Words:

There are several Scriptural references to God who will:

> *render to each person according to his deeds.*
> (Rom. 2:6)

Jesus said:

> *"I will give to each one of you according to your deeds."*
> (Rev. 2:23)

Jesus also warned:

> *"But I tell you that every careless word that people speak, they shall give an accounting for it in the day of judgment."*
> (Matt. 12:36)

These warnings should not be taken lightly. They are clearly stated so that we may know what is ahead.

### Adjusting Our Theology:

If we are saved by grace through faith, what does it mean

## The Coming Judgment Based on Your Deeds

to be saved? What is salvation? From what are we saved?

Most of the Protestant Christians I know think of salvation as God's gift through which an individual is instantly forgiven of their sins and then given the eternal reward of heaven. Of course, it is true that our sins are forgiven and we Christian are guaranteed a place of eternal happiness with God. But I want to be more specific as to what actually happens with salvation.

First, consider what happened to humanity as a result of Adam's sin:

> *Therefore, just as through one man sin entered into the world, and death through sin, and so death spread to all men, because all sinned.*
> (Rom. 5:12)

Because of Adam's sin, all of humanity came under the influence of sin and death. As a consequence, we all sin and we all will die.

Knowing this, we can say that when we put our faith in Jesus we are saved from the power of sin and death.

This aspect of salvation is explained in the Bible in many different ways. We can say that sin no longer rules over us (Rom. 6:18, 22). We are transferred from the realm of darkness and brought into the kingdom of light (Col. 1:13). Jesus is now Lord. Although death is still our enemy, the sting of death has been taken away (I Cor. 15:55-57), and the life of God is in us (I John 5:12), ensuring us that we will be resurrected from the dead (I Cor. 15:51-52).

So far I have listed benefits of salvation without saying anything about the future judgment day. Indeed, salvation does have implications for the coming judgment. In particular, we know that all who put their faith in Jesus *"shall be saved from the wrath of God"* (Rom. 5:9). Hallelujah! Once we

## Defining Salvation

have placed our faith in Jesus we can know without a doubt that God will not unleash any of His anger toward us.

Furthermore, we can note that salvation brings us into the family of God. He adopts us and breathes His Spirit into us (Gal. 4:4-6). We become children of God (John 1:12). We become partakers of divine nature (II Peter 1:4). We are granted eternal life (I John 5:11). And finally, we will be welcomed into a place of eternal happiness with Jesus (John 14:3).

So the benefits of salvation include the following:

- Freed from the power of sin;
- Transferred from Satan's realm to the kingdom of God;
- Delivered from the wrath of God at judgment day;
- Made children of God;
- Became partakers of divine nature;
- Granted eternal life;
- Guaranteed a place of eternal happiness with Jesus.

Is it possible to receive all of these benefits through salvation and still have a future judgment based on deeds? Yes. Think about a father who gathers into his home all of his children so he can share his belongings. He only allows his children to come and all others are refused entrance. Then the father gives to each of his children according to how they have acted and what they have achieved. He can both discipline and reward his children. He loves each and everyone of them, but he deals with them according to their deeds.

In similar fashion we can envision a future judgment for Christians based on deeds. We are presently saved from the power of sin and death. We will be saved from the wrath of God at judgment day. But we will also be recompensed according to our deeds done in the body, whether good or bad.

## Chapter 5
# Good Deeds Are Good

### Rewards Determined by How One Uses Their Talents:

Jesus compared judgment to a master who had entrusted three servants with different talents and then returned to see what they had done with their talents:

> *"Now after a long time the master of those slaves came and settled accounts with them. The one who had received the five talents came up and brought five more talents, saying, 'Master, you entrusted five talents to me. See, I have gained five more talents.' His master said to him, 'Well done, good and faithful slave. You were faithful with a few things, I will put you in charge of many things; enter into the joy of your master.'*
>
> *Also the one who had received the two talents came up and said, 'Master, you entrusted two talents to me. See, I have gained two more talents.' His master said to him, 'Well done, good and faithful slave. You were faithful with a few things, I will put you in charge of many things; enter into the joy of your master.'*
>
> *And the one also who had received the one talent came up and said, 'Master, I knew you to be hard*

# The Coming Judgment Based on Your Deeds

> *man, reaping where you did not sow and gathering where you scattered no seed. And I was afraid, and went away and hid your talent in the ground. See, you have what is yours.'*
>
> *But his master answered and said to him, 'You wicked, lazy slave, you knew that I reap where I did not sow and gather where I scattered no seed. Then you ought to have put my money in the bank, and on my arrival I would have received my money back with interest. Therefore take away the talent from him, and give it to the one who has the ten talents.'*
>
> *For to everyone who has, more shall be given, and he will have an abundance; but from the one who does not have, even what he does have shall be taken away."*
>
> (Matt. 25:19-29)

This indicates a future judgment based on deeds, with rewards being given to us according to how we have used our talents. This seems to indicate that we will be judged according to all that God has given to us, including talents, resources, gifts, abilities and wisdom.

## Adjusting Our Theology:

Some Christians cannot accept this and other passages talking about a judgment based on deeds because they have an extremely negative attitude concerning deeds.

The negative view of deeds became especially seated into Western Christianity during the Protestant Reformation. Leaders of the Reformation such as Martin Luther and John Calvin saw the established Church as teaching people that they must earn their way to heaven by doing good deeds.

## Good Deeds Are Good

Luther and Calvin violently opposed that teaching and determined to proclaim the truth that salvation is given to us by grace rather than works (or deeds).

We can be grateful to Luther and Calvin for what they contributed to Christianity, but today we can see some of their mistakes. In reference to our understanding of salvation and the place of our own deeds, Luther concluded that everything a person does before they become Christian is totally selfish and, therefore, sin. John Calvin expressed a similar belief, writing:

> all human works, if judged according to their own worth, are nothing but filth and defilement. And what is commonly reckoned righteousness is before God sheer iniquity.[2]

One of the Scriptures which teachers of the Protestant Reformation used to teach that all of our deeds are evil and therefore rejected by God is Isaiah 64:6:

> *For all of us have become like one who is unclean,*
> *And all our righteous deeds are like a filthy garment...*

The Reformers took this verse and applied it to all humanity, teaching that before we become Christians we are all unclean and all of our righteous deeds—all of the things we do to try to please God—are rejected by God.

In reality, the Reformers were taking Isaiah 64:6 out of context and twisting the meaning originally intended by the author. Please consider this. Isaiah was writing about the condition of his own people, the Jews, at a time when they were being taken out of Israel and exiled to Babylon. The

---

[2] John Calvin: *Institutes of the Christian Religion,* Library of Christian Classics, ed. by John T. McNeil and trans. by F. L. Battles, 2 vols. (Philadelphia: Westminster, 1960), 3.12.4.

## The Coming Judgment Based on Your Deeds

Jews had been so rebellious to God that God was allowing them to be punished. The Jews were not always rejected by God. There was a time when they had God's favor. He once accepted their offerings and sacrifices, but they had arrived at a time in history when God was no longer accepting their righteous deeds.

Once we realize that Isaiah was writing about a specific group of people, at a specific time in history, we can see how wrong it is to apply Isaiah 64:6 to every human being throughout history. It is *not* true that all of our righteousness deeds are as a filthy garment.

To confirm that God does not reject everyone's righteous deeds all we have to do is read one verse earlier:

*You meet him who rejoices in doing righteousness...*
(Is. 64:5)

God loves it when a mother takes care of her children. He is pleased when a father works to provide for his family. He rejoices when government leaders act righteously.

In other words, good deeds are good. They are not filthy garments in God's eyes.

Of course, no one does enough good deeds to get to heaven. Everyone needs Jesus Christ. No one is perfect. Everyone sins. However, people can do good deeds and God does take note of those good deeds. In fact, He has books with all of our deeds, good and bad, recorded (Rev. 20:12).

## Chapter 6
# Jesus' Righteousness Credited to Us

### Rewards for Good Leaders, Disciples and Overcomers

In addition to the general promises to reward each person for their work, the Bible tells us about specific crowns given to individuals for specific reasons. In I Corinthians 9:24-25, Paul talks about an imperishable crown being given to those who discipline themselves and work diligently. In I Peter 5:1-4, we read about a crown of glory being given to leaders who shepherd with eagerness and show themselves as good examples.

When Peter asked Jesus what reward will be awaiting for him and the other disciples on judgment day, Jesus responded and said:

> "Truly I say to you, that you who have followed Me, in the regeneration when the Son of Man will sit on His glorious throne, you also shall sit upon twelve thrones..."
>
> (Matt. 19:28)

In the Book of Revelation, we can also read how Jesus promised to reward those who overcome in this life:

# The Coming Judgment Based on Your Deeds

> *"He who overcomes, and he who keeps My deeds until the end, to him I will give authority over the nations."*
>
> (Rev. 2:26)

> *"He who overcomes, I will grant to him to sit down with Me on My throne, as I also overcame and sat down with My Father on His throne."*
>
> (Rev. 3:21)

Make no mistake, there will be great authority and positions of prominence granted to those who overcome trials and temptations—for those who continue in obedience to Jesus in difficult circumstances.

## Adjusting Our Theology:

Some Christians cannot accept this idea of differing rewards because they have been taught that the righteousness of Jesus is given to us and we will only be judged based on His righteousness. If God looks at us and only sees Jesus, then we will all be judged perfect and equally deserving of God's blessings. On the other hand, if Christians are going to receive different crowns, rewards, thrones and authority as the above verses tell us, then we need to re-evaluate our theological understanding concerning how the righteousness of Jesus benefits us.

The King James Version of Romans 4 talks about how righteousness was "imputed" to Abraham (vs. 22). Paul goes on to say that the same benefit is available to all of us who put our faith in Jesus:

> *Now it was not written for his sake alone, that it was imputed to him. But for us also, to whom it*

## Jesus' Righteousness Credited to Us

*shall be imputed, if we believe on him that raised up Jesus our Lord from the dead.*
(Rom. 4:23-24, KJV)

From this, we know that righteousness will be imputed to us who believe in Jesus.

Unfortunately, there are two different definitions of our English word "imputed." It can mean "credited to" or "imparted to." We can expound upon these two definitions with synonyms.

Definition #1: credited to, reckoned to or accounted to
Definition #2: imparted to, placed upon or deposited into

Was the righteousness of Jesus credited to us or was it imparted to us?

When we study this more carefully we discover that the word "imputed" was translated from the Greek word, *logizomai*. This Greek word actually means "credited to," not "imparted to." Knowing this, most modern Bible translators have used the word "credited" (or a synonym). For example, the New American Standard says:

*"Therefore it was also credited to him as righteousness."*
(Rom. 4:22)

Paul goes on to explain how Abraham was credited with righteousness, not for his sake only, *"but for our sake also, to whom it will be credited..."* (Rom. 4:24). So then, righteousness is credited to us when we put our faith in Jesus.

This definition of *logizomai* can be confirmed by reading Romans 4:8 (KJV):

## The Coming Judgment Based on Your Deeds

> *Blessed is the man to whom the Lord will not impute sin.*

It makes no sense that God would "impart" sin to a person. So again, we see that the definition of *logizomai* as used in Romans 4 is better translated as "credited to."

To see the difference between "credited to" and "imparted to" consider an analogy. A young man wanted to attend a big sports event in an arena. It just so happened that the older brother of this young man was the owner of the arena. As the younger brother sought entrance, the guards recognized him as the brother of the owner, and so they allowed him free passage. He was credited with the right of passage because of his older brother, but the older brother did not impart his rights to the younger brother. In a similar way, Christians are credited with the righteousness of Jesus and, as a result, we will be allowed free passage into a place of eternal happiness with God.

This truth is so key that we need to dedicate one more chapter to further develop it.

## Chapter 7
# The Individual Christian's Righteousness

### Great Rewards for those Who Suffer and Sacrifice

Consider these promises of Jesus:

> *"Blessed are you when men hate you, and ostracize you, and insult you, and scorn your name as evil, for the sake of the Son of Man. Be glad in that day and leap for joy, for behold, your reward is great in heaven."*
> (Luke 6:22-23)

> *"But when you give a reception, invite the poor, the crippled, the lame, the blind, and you will be blessed, ... you will be repaid at the resurrection of the righteous."*
> (Luke 14:13-14)

> *"And everyone who has left houses or brothers or sisters or father or mother or children or farms for My name's sake, will receive many times as much and will inherit eternal life."*
> (Matt. 19:29)

# The Coming Judgment Based on Your Deeds

What do we learn from these passages? Great rewards await those who suffer for Christ's sake.

## Adjusting Our Theology:

How can judgment be based on the deeds listed above if God looks at us and all He sees is Jesus? Because He doesn't just see Jesus. God actually sees us. *We* will stand before the judgment seat. It is true that we have been credited with the righteousness of Jesus but we will still stand before the judgment seat with our own righteousness or lack thereof. Please let me explain.

The KJV of II Corinthians 5:21 says:

> *For he hath made him to be sin for us, who knew no sin; that we might be made the righteousness of God in him.*

At first reading, this seems to be explaining corresponding actions: our sin is transferred to Jesus as His righteousness is transferred to us. In reality, the phrase, *"we might be made the righteousness of God,"* does not specify *when* a person is made the righteousness of God.

The New American Standard says it a little more clearly:

> *He made Him who knew no sin to be sin on our behalf, so that we might become the righteousness of God in Him.*
>
> (II Cor. 5:21)

Notice the phrase, *"we might become the righteousness of God"* indicates an action which may take place over time and in the future. These verb tenses are accurately translated from the original Greek manuscripts.

## The Individual Christian's Righteousness

This means that we are not yet the righteousness of Jesus. You and I have been credited with the righteousness of Jesus, but we are now in the process of becoming the righteousness of God in Jesus.

This is the only understanding which agrees with other Bible verses talking about each Christian having their own level of righteousness. For example, John wrote:

> *If we confess our sins, He is faithful and righteous to forgive us our sins and to cleanse us from all unrighteousness.*
> (I John 1:9)

Notice that we are in an ongoing process of cleansing from unrighteousness. The writer of Hebrews explained the function of discipline in causing us to grow:

> *it yields the peaceful fruit of righteousness.*
> (Heb. 12:11)

Notice that the Christian's state of righteousness increases as he or she confesses personal sins and matures under the discipline of God.

We know that no one is perfectly righteous apart from Jesus Christ. Romans 3:10 tells us: *"There is none righteous, not even one."* However, in this verse the righteousness being referred to is perfection. Only Jesus meets that standard.

But in Bible times the word "righteousness" did not always refer to the perfect righteousness of Jesus. It was a common word in Bible days and it was used by the common person in everyday language. The word "righteousness" was not coined by Christians, but it had been used for centuries. It referred to "a quality of being right and just." Any person who was just in their dealings with others was consider righteous.

# The Coming Judgment Based on Your Deeds

Even Jesus used the word "righteousness" to refer to a quality of being right, without referring to perfect righteousness. For example, Jesus said,

> *For I say to you that unless your righteousness surpasses that of the scribes and Pharisees, you will not inherit the kingdom of heaven.*
> (Matt. 5:20)

Jesus refers to *"your righteousness"* and the *"righteousness of the scribes and Pharisees."* Of course, your righteousness is not as great as the righteousness of Jesus. Nor was the righteousness of the scribes and Pharisee as great as the righteousness of Jesus. Further we know that the perfect righteousness of Jesus is necessary for a person to experience the kingdom of heaven. But we must not miss the point that Jesus did recognize some quality of righteousness in the lives of His listeners and in the lives of the scribes and Pharisees.

Acknowledging that the word "righteousness" did not necessarily mean perfection in Bible days, we can understand why some non-Christians in the Bible are referred to as righteous—not in the sense of perfection, but indeed possessing some quality of being right. Luke wrote about a man named Joseph, *"who was a member of the Council, a good and righteous man"* (Luke 23:50). A Gentile named Cornelius was said to be, *"...a righteous and God-fearing man..."* (Acts 10:22). Note how the Bible describes Zacharias and Elizabeth:

> *They were both righteous in the sight of God, walking blamelessly in all of the commandments and requirements of the Lord.*
> (Luke 1:6)

Neither Zacharias nor Elizabeth were Christians. Yet they

## The Individual Christian's Righteousness

are said to be righteous. In Matthew 23:35, Jesus refers to all of the righteous people from righteous Adam to righteous Zechariah, implying that there were numerous people in Old Testament times who were righteous.

Let me repeat that no person is perfectly righteous. No one will get to heaven unless they have been credited with the perfect righteousness of Jesus Christ. However, each person has their own level of righteousness and each person will stand before the judgment seat and *"give an account of himself to God"* (Rom. 14:12).

## Chapter 8
# Relational, Not Legal, Understanding

### Judgment Will Be Harsher for Some than Others:

There are some passages in the Bible which indicate that judgment will be harsher for some Christians than others.

> *Let not many of you become teachers, my brethren, knowing that as such we will incur a stricter judgment.*
> (James 3:1)

> *"From everyone who has been given much, much will be required; and to whom they entrusted much, of him they will ask all the more."*
> (Luke 12:48)

### Adjusting Our Theology:

Many Christians have no theological context in which they can fit a judgment of varying degrees because they have a *legalized* understanding of judgment. When I say this, I am not referring to legalism in the sense of obeying laws in order to be saved. Instead, I am referring to how certain Protestant

# The Coming Judgment Based on Your Deeds

leaders understood salvation like a legal transaction which takes place in a courtroom.

Before I explain this, let me review the benefits of salvation which we received when we placed our faith in Jesus:

- Freed from the power of sin;
- Transferred from Satan's realm to the kingdom of God;
- Delivered from the wrath of God at judgment day;
- Made children of God;
- Became partakers of divine nature;
- Granted eternal life;
- Guaranteed a place of eternal happiness with God.

These benefits are given to us by grace, on no merit of our own. There is nothing we can do to earn them. Furthermore, there is nothing we can do to gain God's love. He loved us even while we were sinners and He will never leave us nor forsake us.

Even though I recognize these benefits, I am not including the all-or-nothing idea that all Christians receive the same rewards in heaven. I am challenging the teaching that says when God looks at us, all He sees is Jesus. We will individually stand before God and give an account for our own deeds.

As I mentioned, confusion on this subject sometimes stems from a legalized understanding of judgment. This is especially true with the teachings of John Calvin. Before he reoriented his life to studying and teaching theology, he was a lawyer. It was only natural for Calvin to understand theology in legal terms. He saw the salvation experience as a legal exchange: our sin placed upon Jesus and His righteousness placed upon us.[3] Each person will stand in the courtroom of

---

[3] This idea was expressed many times by Calvin; e.g., John Calvin: *Institutes of the Christian Religion,* Library of Christian Classics, ed. by John T. McNeil and trans. by F. L. Battles, 2 vols. (Philadelphia: Westminster,

## Relational, Not Legal, Understanding

God, with or without the righteousness of Jesus. John Calvin reasoned that those without Jesus' righteousness will experience the wrath of God and be sentenced to eternal damnation. Those with the righteousness of Jesus will receive the fullness of God's blessings.

Reinforcing this legal understanding is how many Protestants today define certain terms. For example, righteousness is sometimes defined as "right standing with God." This definition portrays the individual as standing erect before God—even standing in a courtroom before the Great Judge. This goes back to the legal understanding of salvation in which many of the Protestant reformers developed their theology.

In order to understand the biblical terms properly we must see them in a relational context, rather than a legal context. In a courtroom people are declared guilty or innocent. In God's courtroom people will be declared as guilty or forgiven. There is a significant difference. We should not think of Jesus in the same way we think of a regular judge who rules from his bench. This Judge has love in His eyes. He is not merely passing a judgment based on law. When Jesus sees one of His own, He will come down from the bench, take him into His arms and tell him that He has taken care of the charges.

Remember how our Lord described judgment day in Matthew 25:34:

> "Then the King will say to those on His right, 'Come, you who are blessed of My Father, inherit the kingdom prepared for you from the foundation of the world.'"

This is a picture of Jesus welcoming us into God's presence and treating us like family. He is not merely sending us away

---

1960), 3.12.2 and 9.

# The Coming Judgment Based on Your Deeds

to heaven or hell. He is taking us into His arms and bringing us into His home.

This image of judgment is in keeping with the parable Jesus told of the prodigal son. Jesus did not tell of a father who drug his wayward son off to the courtroom. Instead, the father ran to his son, embraced him and brought him home (Luke 15:11-24).

So also, when we appear before the judgment seat of God, we will be shown compassion. We will not be declared guilty or innocent. Instead, we will be treated as forgiven. We will be treated as the Judge's family members. We will be welcomed into the presence of the Father and be recompensed for our deeds.

## Chapter 9

# Not All Sins Are Equal

### Rewards for the Humble

Jesus said that *"many who are first will be last; and the last, first"* (Matt. 19:30). By this He was referring to how many people who seem to be successful, worthy of great rewards and even holy in this life, will be demoted to positions of less notoriety and honor in heaven. Some of this reversal will be because they did their good deeds to be noticed by others. Jesus explained:

> *"Beware of practicing your righteousness before men to be noticed by them; otherwise you have no reward with your Father who is in heaven. So when you give to the poor do not sound a trumpet before you, as the hypocrites do in the synagogues and in the streets, so that they may be honored by men. Truly I say to you, they have their reward in full. But when you give to the poor, do not let your left hand know what your right hand is doing, so that your giving will be in secret; and your Father who sees what is done in secret will reward you."*
> (Matt. 6:1-4)

Jesus mentions the same concept about prayer (vs 5-6) and

# The Coming Judgment Based on Your Deeds

fasting (vs 16-18). Our rewards will be based upon our attitude and whether or not we did those deeds to gain the praise of others.

## Adjusting Our Theology:

Jesus' teaching that some will be first while others will be last is contrary to the idea of judgment being based only on our acceptance or rejection of Jesus Christ. Of course, Jesus is the only way to the Father. But we must realize that there remains a judgment which will result in some being first and others last.

Many Christians have a hard time accepting this because their legalized understanding of judgment leads them to see every person as guilty or innocent. Furthermore, they see every person as equally guilty until they have received Jesus Christ. This idea of "equally guilty" is sometimes taught from a distorted understanding of James 2:10:

> *For whoever keeps the whole law and yet stumbles in one point, he has become guilty of all.*

Some teachers use this verse to emphasize how every person is equally guilty no matter if their sins are very serious or not so serious. They are trying to drive home the truth that everyone is guilty and needs the forgiveness available through Jesus Christ.

Of course, salvation is only available through Jesus. Of course, everyone sins. But James 2:10 was not saying that every sin is equally bad. On the contrary, James was exhorting his followers not to live by the Jewish Laws in the Old Testament because if a person errs in one little area, they are held guilty of all the Jewish Laws. In saying this, James was not telling his listeners to try keep all of the Jewish Laws;

## Not All Sins Are Equal

he was saying that Christians should not even try live by the Jewish Laws. Instead, James exhorted them to live by *"the royal law according to the Scripture, 'You shall love your neighbor as yourself' "* (James 2:8). In other words: if you try to live by the Jewish Laws, you must keep each and every Law in order to be perfect. But Christians should not even try live by those Laws, because we have a new and greater law which is to love our neighbors as ourselves.

Since we Christians are not to live by the Jewish Laws, it is *not* true that whoever *"stumbles in one point, he has become guilty of all."* That does not apply to us. That applies to people trying to live by the Jewish Laws. Jesus fulfilled the Jewish Laws for us, and therefore, those Laws are set aside. It is not the standard by which we will be judged.

However, there is a new law which does apply to us. We will be judged by the law which Jesus gave to us—to love God with our whole heart and our neighbor as ourself. According to this law of love, we will be evaluated based on what we have actually done. We are not equally guilty. Nor are we equally deserving of rewards. In fact, we will be judged according to how we have acted in love towards those around us.

## Chapter 10
# A Works-Oriented Life

### Rewards Determined by How One Builds the Church:

Paul explained how judgment day will reveal the quality of the Christians' labor in reference to building the Church:

> *According to the grace of God which was given to me, like a wise master builder I laid a foundation, and another is building on it. But each man must be careful how he builds on it. For no man can lay a foundation other than the one which is laid, which is Jesus Christ. Now if any man builds on the foundation with gold, silver, precious stones, wood, hay, straw, each man's work will become evident; for the day will show it because it is to be revealed with fire, and the fire itself will test the quality of each man's work. If any man's work which he has built on it remains, he will receive a reward. If any man's work is burned up, he will suffer loss; but he himself will be saved, yet so as through fire.*
>
> (I Cor. 3:10-15)

Notice it is one thing to be saved, it is another to receive rewards. Salvation is given to all those who believe in Jesus.

# The Coming Judgment Based on Your Deeds

Rewards are given according to the quality of each person's work in building up the Church.

## **Adjusting Our Theology:**

If we believe these words of Paul, there is no doubt that a future judgment based on deeds is ahead of us. Yet, some Christians still avoid talking about it. They are concerned that their Christianity will become a "works-oriented religion." They think that focusing on coming rewards will pervert their Christianity.

Will our Christianity become a works-oriented religion? Nowhere in this book have I said or even hinted that we can work for our salvation. It is given to us by grace through faith. Nor can we successfully work for God's love. He loves us just as we are.

But each of us will still be judged according to our deeds. Does that make it a works-oriented religion?

To answer this we should first note that the word "religion" can make the phrase, "works-oriented religion," sound bad to Christians who have negative attitudes about the rules and regulations imposed by some religious leaders. But if we use the word "religion" properly we can say as James did:

> *Pure and undefiled religion in the sight of our God and Father is this: to visit orphans and widows in the their distress, and to keep oneself unstained by the world.*
>
> (James 1:27)

This type of works-oriented religion is not bad. I dare say that we should work. *We should have a works-orientation to our lives.* Furthermore, we should be concerned about judgment day and what eternal rewards await us.

# A Works-Oriented Life

Think about this:

1. Why did Jesus tell us of a coming judgment during which He will select those who cared for the hungry, thirsty, stranger, naked, sick and imprisoned?
2. Why did Paul write that we will all appear before the judgment seat of Christ and each one will be recompensed for his deeds in the body, according to what he has done, whether good or bad?
3. Then again, why did Paul warn Christians that we will all stand before the judgment seat of God and each one of us will give an account of himself to God?
4. Why did Jesus tell the parable explaining that judgment day will be like a master returning and demanding his servants to show what they had done with their talents?
5. Why does the Bible tell us about crowns, rewards and authority that will be given to overcomers?
6. Why did Jesus promise rewards to those who sacrifice and suffer for His sake?
7. Why did Paul explain to Christians that judgment day will reveal the quality of their labors in building the Church?

The answer is simple: to motivate us.

Will this motivation for works pervert our Christianity? Quite the opposite. Any form of Christianity that does not recognize a coming judgment based on deeds is already perverted and needs to be straightened out.

Of course, sincere believers could take this to extremes thinking that they must turn into Mother Teresa. Some may fall into condemnation convinced that they are never doing enough. Worse yet, some Church leaders could use teachings about the coming judgment to manipulate people. The re-

## The Coming Judgment Based on Your Deeds

sults of focusing too much on the rewards that await us may compel some people to sell everything, give to the poor and become neurotic do-gooders.

Yes, it is true that an over-emphasis on the coming judgment may lead Christians into a mode of life which is too performance oriented. But on the other hand, denying the coming judgment can lead to a passivity and allow many to lose themselves in a self-oriented life, spending all of their days in pleasures and accumulating material possessions for themselves. Furthermore, never teaching about a coming judgment may lead to a day when Christians stand before Jesus, having done nothing for the poor, needy, orphans, widows, sick and imprisoned.

Some Christians still will not accept this, claiming that all of our works should be motivated by love for God rather than the rewards we will receive. Of course, love should be at the foundation of our lives and deeds. But think how parents raise their children. It would be nice if children would keep their bedrooms clean just because they love their parents, but every parent knows that that is not going to happen. Children need some added incentive and there is nothing wrong with added incentive. It is why the Bible tells us about the rewards awaiting us.

Consider Jesus, *"who for the joy set before Him endured the cross"* (Heb. 12:2). Just as Jesus did, we should endure and sacrifice during this life, so that we may enjoy greater blessings in the next life.

# Conclusion

So there is a test ahead of us. What is on the test? What will the Judge be looking for?

We have several Bible verses giving us general warnings that God will render to every person according to their deeds. These statements seem to imply that *everything* we have done will be taken into account. Yet, it sounds like the sins we confess while alive will be forgiven and we will be cleansed from the related unrighteousness. Therefore, these will be removed from the list of things for which we will be held accountable.

There are also specific Bible passages which tell us about deeds which God will take special notice of:

1. Whether or not we cared for the hungry, thirsty, stranger, naked, sick and imprisoned;
2. How we have used or not used the talents and resources which He has given to us;
3. Whether or not we overcame the obstacles, trials and persecutions we face;
4. How we sacrificed and suffered for Christ's sake;
5. The quality of our work in building up the body of Christ.

Notice that each of these are real deeds—not just vague standards of holiness or keeping a set of rules such as not smoking, drinking or overeating. Of course, negative behav-

# The Coming Judgment Based on Your Deeds

iors are included in the general exhortations that tell us we will each be judged according to whatever we have done. But the primary focus on judgment day will be on actual deeds towards our neighbors, Christian brothers and sisters, and the Church.

Plus our rewards will be determined by our heart motivations. Those who did good deeds to be noticed by others will have already received their rewards in full. Those who did good deeds simply to honor and please the Father will be greatly rewarded by Him.

How then should you live? If, indeed, your deeds will be taken into account on judgment day, then you should be living with that in mind. Of course, you do not need to become neurotic about doing good deeds, but hopefully you will do something. Even doing something simple is better than doing nothing. Visit the imprisoned. Volunteer at the local homeless shelter. Contribute time and finances to your church. Start giving. Cultivate a lifestyle of caring for the needy. Sponsor an orphan. Bless a widow. Support a missionary. Dedicate a portion of your income to those who are suffering. Get the flow started. Your heart will go where your treasure is and you will fall in love with the people you help. Then maybe you will grow in your love and soon you will be God's hand and heart reaching out to the sick and imprisoned, weak and naked, orphans and widows. You have certain gifts, abilities and resources. Use what you have. Do your part and you will be blessed both in this life and the next.

The last words of Jesus recorded in the Bible are these:

*"Behold, I am coming quickly, and My reward is with Me, to render to every man according to what he has done... I, Jesus, have sent My angel to testify to you these things for the churches. I am the root and the descendant of David, the bright morning star... Yes, I am coming quickly."*
(Rev. 22:14-22)

These are sobering words. They are meant to be sobering. They are meant to be motivating.

## Other Books by Harold R. Eberle

### Christianity Unshackled

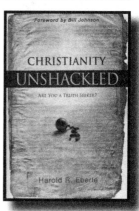

Most Christians in the Western world have no idea how profoundly their beliefs have been influenced by their culture. What would Christianity be like, if it was separated from Western thought? After untangling the Western traditions of the last 2,000 years of Church history, Harold R. Eberle offers a Christian worldview that is clear, concise, and liberating. This will shake you to the core and then leave you standing on a firm foundation!

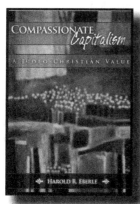

### Compassionate Capitalism: A Judeo-Christian Value

As you read this book, you will learn how capitalism first developed as God worked among the Hebrew people in the Old Testament. The resulting economic principles then transformed Western society as they spread with Christianity. However, our present form of capitalism is different than that which God instilled in Hebrew society. What we need to do now is govern capitalism wisely and apply the principles of capitalism with compassion.

### Releasing Kings into the Marketplace for Ministry

By John Garfield and Harold R. Eberle

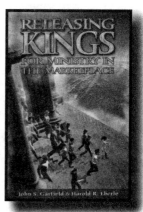

"Kings" is what we call Christian leaders who have embraced the call of God upon their life to work in the marketplace and from that position transform society. This book explains how marketplace ministry will operate in concert with local churches and pastors. It provides a Scriptural basis for the expansion of the Kingdom of God into all areas of society.

# Other Books by Harold R. Eberle

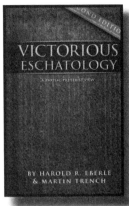

## Victorious Eschatology
Co-authored by
Harold R. Eberle and Martin Trench

Here it is—a biblically-based, optimistic view of the future. Along with a historical perspective, this book offers a clear understanding of Matthew 24, the book of Revelation, and other key passages about the events to precede the return of Jesus Christ. Satan is not going to take over this world. Jesus Christ is Lord and He will reign until every enemy is put under His feet!

## Jesus Came Out of the Tomb...So Can You!
*A Brief Explanation of Resurrection-based Christianity*

Forgiveness of sins is at the cross. Power over sin is in the resurrection and ascension. If God raised Jesus from the tomb in power and glory, then we can experience that resurrection power. If God raised Jesus into heaven, and us with Him, then we can live in His victory!

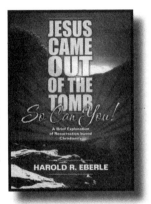

## Developing a Prosperous Soul
**Vol. I: How to Overcome a Poverty Mind-set**
**Vol. II: How to Move into God's Financial Blessings**

There are fundamental changes you can make in the way you think which will help you release God's blessings. This is a balanced look at the promises of God with practical steps you can take to move into financial freedom. It is time for Christians to recapture the financial arena. These two volumes will inspire and create faith in you to fulfill God's purpose for your life.

# Other books by Harold R. Eberle

## Living and Dying with the King James Bible

The King James Version (KJV) has been a gift of God to the Body of Christ. It has been the standard of truth and inspiration which has stabilized the Protestant Church and blessed millions of people. But someone needs to say it: the KJV is an inferior translation. In these pages, Harold R. Eberle clearly shows the errors and biases of the KJV, hoping you will consider the advantages of more modern Bible translations.

## The Complete Wineskin
(Fourth edition)

The Body of Christ is in a reformation. God is pouring out His Holy Spirit and our wineskins must be changed to handle the new wine. Will the Church come together in unity? How does the anointing of God work and what is your role? What is the 5-fold ministry? How are apostles, prophets, evangelists, pastors, and teachers going to rise up and work together? Where do small group meetings fit in? This book puts into words what you have been sensing in your spirit. (Eberle's best seller, translated into many languages, distributed worldwide.)

## God's Leaders for Tomorrow's World
(Revised/expanded edition)

You sense the call to leadership, but questions persist: "Does God want me to rise up? Do I truly know where to lead? Is this pride? How can I influence people?" Through an understanding of leadership dynamics, learn how to develop godly charisma. Confusion will melt into order when you see the God-ordained lines of authority. Fear of leadership will change to confidence as you learn to handle power struggles. It is time to move into your "metron," that is, your God-given sphere of authority.

# Other Books by Harold R. Eberle

## Two Become One
(Second edition)
*Releasing God's Power for Romance, Sexual Freedom and Blessings in Marriage*

The keys to a thrilling, passionate, and fulfilling marriage can be yours if you want them. Kindle afresh the "buzz of love." Find out how to make God's law of binding forces work for you rather than against you. This book is of great benefit to pastors, counselors, young singles, divorces, and especially married people. Couples are encouraged to read it together.

## Grace...the Power to Reign
*The Light Shining from Romans 5-8*

We struggle against sin and yearn for God's highest. Yet, on a bad day it is as if we are fighting against gravity. Questions go unanswered:
- Where is the power to overcome temptations and trials?
- Is God really willing to breathe into us that these dry bones can live and we may stand strong?

For anyone who has ever struggled to live godly, here are the answers.

## Who Is God?

Challenging the traditional Western view of God, Harold R. Eberle presents God as a Covenant-maker, Lover, and Father. Depending on Scripture, God is shown to be in a vulnerable, open, and cooperative relationship with His people. This book is both unsettling and enlightening—revolutionary to most readers—considered by many to be Harold's most important contribution to the Body of Christ.

## Other Books by Harold R. Eberle

### The Spiritual, Mystical and Supernatural
(Second edition)

In this book, Harold explains the spiritual realm from a Christian perspective. He deals with issues such as: what exists in the spiritual realm; how people access that realm; discerning things in the spirit; activities of witches, psychics and New Agers; spiritual impartations and influences between people; out-of-body experiences; interpretation of dreams; angelic and demonic visitations; understanding supernatural phenomena from a biblical perspective.

### Precious In His Sight
(Third edition)
*A Fresh Look at the Nature of Humanity*

What happened when Adam sinned? How does that sin influence us? Where do babies go if they die? How evil are we? How can I love myself if I am evil? These subjects have far-reaching implications, including our understanding of ourselves, our neighbors, sin, salvation, how we evangelize and how we live the daily victorious life.

---

**To place an order or to check current prices on these and other books, call:**

**1-800-308-5837 within the USA or**
**509-248-5837 from outside of the USA**

Worldcast Publishing
P.O. Box 10653
Yakima, WA 98909-1653

E-mail: office@worldcastpublishing.com
Web Site: www.worldcastpublishing.com